Original title:
The Insightful Heart

Copyright © 2024 Book Fairy Publishing
All rights reserved.

Author: Samira Siil
ISBN HARDBACK: 978-9916-87-366-3
ISBN PAPERBACK: 978-9916-87-367-0
ISBN EBOOK: 978-9916-87-368-7

Where Intuition Meets Emotion

In quiet moments, wisdom stirs,
Gentle whispers, the heart's soft purrs.
Feelings rise like dawn's first light,
Guiding dreams into the night.

Paths entwined, the journey grows,
Within the heart, the truth bestows.
The mind's still calm, the soul's embrace,
In sacred space, we find our grace.

Shadows that Embrace the Soul

Late at night, secrets dwell,
In the dark, we hear the bell.
Shadows dance, a silent plea,
Whispers weave our destiny.

Holding hands with fear and fate,
In the void, we contemplate.
The soul's echoes, soft and low,
Guide us where the rivers flow.

Tides of Tenderness

Waves of love crash on the shore,
Gentle rhythms, forevermore.
In each crest, a beating heart,
Carving dreams, we play our part.

Moonlit paths and starlit skies,
In the depths, our true home lies.
Embracing all that sings and sighs,
In tender tides, our spirit tries.

A Heart that Remembers

In the garden of lost refrain,
Petals fallen, yet there remains.
Moments stitched with threads of gold,
The warmth of stories yet untold.

Faded photographs, timeless grace,
Every heartbeat, a sacred place.
Memories bound in love's own tether,
A heart that remembers, now and forever.

A Symphony of Shared Silence

In quiet moments, we align,
The softest echoes, hearts entwined.
A gentle drift, souls softly hum,
In silence shared, we've just begun.

The world outside fades to a blur,
In this embrace, thoughts softly stir.
With every breath, the stillness sings,
A symphony of quiet springs.

Reflections of a Kindred Spirit

In the mirror of your eyes, I see,
A depth of understanding, you and me.
We share our dreams, our hopes, our fears,
In every glance, a sea of years.

Like gentle waves upon the shore,
Kindred spirits, always wanting more.
In whispers soft, secrets unwind,
In the dance of life, our paths aligned.

Notes from a Caring Heart

With every word, a warmth ignites,
A melody born of starry nights.
You speak, and I hear the soul's refrain,
A heartfelt tune, a gentle rain.

Each note we share builds a bridge,
Across the chasm, our own ridge.
The language spoken with love's own art,
Echoes forever, a caring heart.

Starlit Paths of Shared Understanding

Beneath the stars, we walk as one,
In every silence, stories spun.
The night unfolds, a canvas bright,
With shared understanding, hearts take flight.

The constellations guide our way,
In laughter, tears, night turns to day.
Together, we seek, we find, we grow,
On starlit paths, our spirits glow.

The Quiet Strength of Softness

In whispers soft, the courage grows,
A gentle heart, its power shows.
Like petals bloom in morning light,
With strength they face the coming night.

Through trials faced with tender grace,
Resilience found in each embrace.
A silent force, steadfast and true,
In quiet moments, strength renews.

Threads of Humanity's Pulse

Weaving stories, hearts entwined,
In every thread, a truth we find.
Connected souls in joy and pain,
Together we rise, together we rain.

In laughter shared and tears we shed,
Across the world, our spirits spread.
A tapestry, both rich and vast,
Embracing present, honoring past.

Journeying Through Inner Landscapes

Across the fields of thoughts untamed,
Through valleys deep, my fears are named.
The mountains high, my hopes take flight,
In shadows, I find flickers of light.

Each step I take, the path reveals,
The strength within, the soul it heals.
With every turn, new sights to see,
The landscape shifts, it sets me free.

The Beauty of Gentle Understanding

A quiet nod, a knowing glance,
In simple acts, we find our chance.
Compassion thrives when hearts align,
In gentle ways, the world does shine.

It's in the pause, we gather strength,
With insight shared at any length.
Through soft reflections, wisdom grows,
In understanding, true love flows.

Embracing the Heart's Quietude

In the stillness where time slows,
Whispers of peace gently flow.
Silent thoughts like stars appear,
Embracing calm, I draw near.

A breath held deep, a moment pure,
In quietude, my soul will tour.
The heart becomes a sacred space,
Where love unfolds with gentle grace.

Chasing Shadows of Emotions

Beneath the veil of daylight's grace,
Shadows dance, they leave no trace.
Fleeting moments, joys and fears,
In chasing shadows, life appears.

Emotions rise like tides that sway,
Pulling hearts in bright array.
Yet in the shadows, truths are found,
Where silence speaks without a sound.

The Art of Listening Deeply

In every word, a story breathes,
Between the lines, the heart believes.
Listening close, a precious gift,
In quiet moments, spirits lift.

With open ears and hearts that yearn,
The art of listening, we discern.
For in each pause, and sigh, and glance,
Connections bloom, a timeless dance.

Hidden Treasures of the Heart

In chambers deep, where secrets lie,
Hidden treasures softly sigh.
Love and kindness, wrapped in gold,
Stories waiting to be told.

With gentle hands, I seek and find,
The treasures waiting, intertwined.
In every heartbeat, whispers sing,
A wealth of joy that love can bring.

The Alchemy of Feelings

In shadows deep, emotions stir,
A tapestry of dreams that blur.
Gold and silver, heartbeats blend,
Transforming thoughts, as spirits mend.

Whispers soft, like gentle rain,
Wash away the bitter pain.
In the cauldron, love ignites,
Turning darkness into lights.

Fragments of joy, sorrow's trace,
Dance together in a space.
Alchemy of souls entwined,
From the ashes, hope aligned.

Resonance of True Listening

In silence, hearts begin to speak,
A gentle touch, no need for peek.
Listening close, with open mind,
In the rhythm, truth we find.

Echoes soft, like waves on shore,
Each word shared, brings so much more.
Resonance born through patient eyes,
Breaking walls, where spirit flies.

Understanding blooms in tender care,
Crafted moments, rich and rare.
A bond of trust, woven tight,
In the dark, we bring the light.

Navigating the Currents of Understanding

Life's river flows, both calm and wild,
Weaving paths where dreams are filed.
Charting courses, heart and brain,
Together, through both joy and pain.

Beneath the surface, currents hide,
Pulling us, like an unseen tide.
With every stroke, we learn to steer,
Navigating doubt, facing fear.

With hands united, we set our sails,
Through stormy nights and gentle gales.
Trust the journey, share the load,
In our hearts, a shared abode.

Embers of Kindness

In winter's chill, a spark ignites,
Embers glow in darkest nights.
Kindness spreads, a warming flame,
Turning strangers, to friends by name.

With every smile, the heart expands,
Healing touch, in gentle hands.
Caring whispers, soft as snow,
Bringing light where shadows grow.

Planting seeds of love's embrace,
In every heart, a sacred space.
Embers flicker, then ignite,
Together, we embrace the light.

Harmonies of Unspoken Truths

In silent whispers, hearts collide,
Echoes linger, secrets reside.
A melody woven, soft and rare,
In shadows cast, the truth lays bare.

Fragments of light in the depths we find,
Notes of freedom play, unconfined.
Timid sighs, a gentle embrace,
In the quiet, we find our place.

A Journey Through Shared Sorrows

Together we tread on paths of grief,
With heavy hearts, we seek relief.
Hand in hand through the storms we face,
Finding strength in time and space.

Memories linger, both bitter and sweet,
In the silence, our spirits meet.
Every tear a story, every laugh a song,
In shared sorrows, we grow strong.

The Pulse of Awareness

In mindful breaths, we come alive,
Each heartbeat whispers, we survive.
Moments slipping through our grasp,
In the now, we find our clasp.

Awareness blooms in gentle light,
Guiding souls through the darkest night.
With open eyes, we see the whole,
In every moment, we find our role.

Beneath the Veil of Emotion

Masked in shadows, feelings hide,
Each tear a tale of love denied.
Curled in silence, whispers ache,
Beneath the surface, hearts can break.

Yet through the layers, warmth remains,
A tapestry of joy and pains.
In vulnerability, we find our way,
Beneath the veil, love's bright array.

The Canvas of Compassionate Moments

In gentle strokes, we touch the heart,
Colors blend, a work of art.
Each shade a story, grief or cheer,
We paint our hopes, we draw them near.

With brush in hand, we lend our grace,
An open smile, a warm embrace.
In silence shared, our spirits rise,
Compassion's glow, a soft surprise.

Upon the Wings of Empathy

Like feathers floating in the air,
We lift each other from despair.
With every word, a gentle touch,
Understanding grows, it means so much.

Together flying, side by side,
Through stormy skies, we will abide.
On wings of hope, we soar and glide,
Empathy's dance, our hearts collide.

The Depths of Uncharted Feelings

Beneath the surface, waters flow,
Unseen currents, ebb and glow.
In shadowed depths, we seek to find,
The hidden truths of the heart and mind.

With every wave, emotions rise,
A tempest stirs beneath the skies.
We navigate through fear and grace,
In these depths, we find our place.

The Pulse of Life's Wisdom

In every heartbeat, life resounds,
A rhythm steady, truth abounds.
Lessons learned in joy and strife,
The pulse unfolds the song of life.

With every whisper, secrets told,
In ages past, in futures bold.
Through moments shared, we come to see,
The wisdom of our unity.

Threads of Thoughtful Awareness

In the quiet of morning light,
Thoughts weave in soft flight.
A tapestry of dreams unfolds,
Stories in whispers told.

Moments dance in gentle sway,
Golden threads guide the way.
Each heartbeat carries a sound,
Awareness in stillness found.

The world breathes in soft hues,
Colors blend, old and new.
In silence, wisdom takes flight,
Threads of thought in the night.

Mindful steps on paths unknown,
With every breath, seeds are sown.
Awareness blooms like spring's delight,
As threads of thought take their flight.

The Rhythm of Unexpressed Feelings

In shadows, feelings lie still,
Echoes of a subtle will.
They flutter like leaves in wind,
A symphony yet to begin.

Heartbeats pulse in quiet space,
Yearnings wrapped in soft embrace.
A tempo felt but never shown,
In silence, they find their tone.

Words dance just beyond the veil,
A story woven, frail and pale.
Each unspoken note resounds,
In the hush, the truth abounds.

The rhythm beats within the soul,
An inner world that feels whole.
With each breath, emotions swell,
In the quiet, we hear them tell.

A Journey to Inner Resilience

Through valleys low and mountains high,
The spirit learns to soar and fly.
Steps taken on uncertain ground,
Strength within starts to be found.

The path is rough, the way unclear,
But resilience draws ever near.
Each stumble shapes the heart and mind,
In struggle, treasures we find.

Sunrise breaks, a new day's call,
With courage, we rise after the fall.
Lessons learned through trials faced,
With each challenge, we're embraced.

The journey winds like a river's flow,
Teaching us to bend, to grow.
In the depths, we find the light,
A resilient heart, shining bright.

Secrets in the Fabric of Being

In the weave of night and day,
Whispers of truth softly play.
Threads of time intertwine and bend,
Secrets that the heart descends.

The fabric holds a silent claim,
Stories stitched without a name.
Patterns formed through joy and strife,
The hidden songs of our life.

In textures rich, we find our place,
Echoes of love in every space.
A gentle touch, a knowing glance,
In the weave, we find our chance.

Beneath the surface, we explore,
The secrets that we can't ignore.
In every thread, a sacred truth,
The fabric of being, a living proof.

Embracing the Unseen

In shadows deep, where whispers lie,
Mysteries weave beneath the sky.
With open hearts, we seek and find,
A world that dances, undefined.

Silent echoes in the night,
Illuminated by soft light.
Each heartbeat sings a hidden song,
Revealing truths where we belong.

Beneath the surface, secrets dwell,
A tapestry that time will tell.
Embrace the unseen, take a chance,
For life unfolds in a gentle dance.

Chronicles of the Heart's Wisdom

Pages worn with tales of old,
Whispers shared and dreams retold.
Each heartbeat marks a written line,
Inked with love, both yours and mine.

Moments treasured, lessons learned,
For every heart, a flame that burned.
Through joy and sorrow, paths entwined,
A bigger picture we will find.

With every tear, a seed is sown,
In the garden of the heart we've grown.
Chronicles penned with steadied hand,
Each memory a cherished strand.

A Dance of Unspoken Truths

In quiet glances, stories bloom,
A world that thrives beyond the room.
Where words might falter, silence speaks,
In gentle motions, love's mystique.

We dance beneath the moonlit gaze,
In realms where understanding lays.
Each movement tells what words can't say,
A language rich in shades of gray.

Unspoken truths, a sacred pact,
A bond created, never lacked.
Through every sway, through every twirl,
Life reveals its hidden pearl.

Songs of a Nurtured Soul

In the cradle of the morning light,
A melody stirs, taking flight.
With tender notes, the heart unfolds,
A symphony of dreams retold.

From whispered winds to rustling trees,
Nature's chorus drifts with ease.
Soft harmonies that lift the spirit,
In every sound, a careful lyric.

Nurtured souls, we rise and sing,
Embracing all that life can bring.
In shared connection, love's embrace,
We find our home in this vast space.

Veils of Compassion

In shadows soft, the whispers rise,
A gentle touch, where kindness lies.
With every heart, a story we weave,
In veils of love, we dare believe.

The world outside, a storm may brew,
Yet warmth within can guide us through.
With open arms, we share the weight,
In compassion's light, we resonate.

Each tear that falls can pave the way,
To brighter dawns and hope's ballet.
As petals fall, new blooms will show,
In veils of grace, our spirits grow.

Palette of Honest Sentiments

In shades of truth, our feelings blend,
Each stroke a tale, emotions mend.
With vibrant hues, we paint the night,
And capture dreams in purest light.

The canvas speaks in silence bold,
In every shade, our hearts unfold.
With careful brush, the moments flow,
A palette rich, where passions glow.

Each color tells a story bright,
Of joy and pain, of wrong and right.
In honesty, we find our place,
In this vast world, a warm embrace.

Murmurs in the Stillness

In quiet hours, the whispers breathe,
A tranquil heart, the soul achieves.
Among the leaves, the secrets sigh,
In stillness deep, we learn to fly.

The gentle breeze, it carries tales,
Of dreams once lost, of distant trails.
In every pause, we hear the call,
Of moments pure that bind us all.

In twilight's glow, our spirits dance,
In echoes soft, we take a chance.
For in the stillness, truth reveals,
The murmurings that time conceals.

The Garden of Kindred Connections

In tender soil, our roots entwine,
A garden blooms, a love divine.
With every seed, a friendship sown,
In kindred hearts, we find our home.

The flowers speak in colors bright,
Of laughter shared and shared delight.
Through seasons change, we stand as one,
In shaded paths, our journeys run.

With every bud, a hope reborn,
In morning's light, the promise sworn.
In unity, we find our grace,
In this warm garden, a sacred space.

When Hearts Speak Freely

In whispered tones, we share our dreams,
The gentle flow of moonlit streams.
With every gaze, our souls entwine,
In this embrace, we redefine.

Words like petals, soft and light,
Beneath the stars, we find our light.
No masks, no walls, just open hearts,
In freed connection, love imparts.

Each laugh a note, each tear a song,
In simple truths, we both belong.
The magic grows in every pause,
When hearts speak freely, we find our cause.

Together we weave a tapestry rare,
In moments cherished, beyond compare.
With every heartbeat, every sigh,
In love's pure essence, we rise and fly.

Illuminated Moments of Connection

In fleeting glances, time stands still,
A spark ignites, a shared thrill.
The world recedes, we find our place,
In illuminated moments, we trace.

The laughter dances upon the air,
A gentle touch, a silent prayer.
Though words are few, our hearts know well,
In every heartbeat, stories dwell.

Through crowded rooms, we find each other,
In smiles exchanged, we feel the cover.
A fleeting moment, yet feels so grand,
In bright connections, we understand.

These moments glow, like stars in night,
A fragile beauty, a shared light.
In every sigh, in every glance,
We touch eternity in our dance.

The Tapestry of Tenderness

Woven threads of gentlest grace,
In every laugh, in every embrace.
We build a bond, both strong and fine,
The tapestry of love, divine.

With colors bright and textures true,
We stitch our lives, just me and you.
Through seasons changing, hand in hand,
In this warm fabric, we boldly stand.

Each moment adds a brilliant hue,
In this soft weave, a story grew.
Through trials faced, through joys we share,
The tapestry holds our fragile care.

In threads of trust and strands of cheer,
We find our solace, hold it near.
A cherished work, forever blessed,
In tenderness, we are expressed.

Unveiling Inner Landscapes

In the quiet depths, we start to see,
The landscapes hidden, wild and free.
With open hearts, we tread the path,
Unveiling dreams, igniting a laugh.

Mountains rise from shared embrace,
An inner world, a sacred space.
Through valleys deep and rivers wide,
In every heartbeat, we confide.

The colors shift, like morning light,
Our spirits dance, taking flight.
In whispered truths, we strip away,
The layers thick, come what may.

In every journey, side by side,
We find the beauty we cannot hide.
Unveiling landscapes, rich and grand,
Together we paint the dreams we planned.

Secrets Carried on the Winds

Whispers dance upon the breeze,
Tales of love and ancient trees.
Carried far from silent shores,
A symphony of secret scores.

In shadows deep, the echoes play,
Softly guiding night and day.
Memories twirl on currents light,
In the heart of the aching night.

Lost in dreams, the voices sing,
Of forgotten hopes they bring.
Through the skies, their stories twine,
In the stillness, they align.

Secrets wrapped in twilight's veil,
On the winds, they tell their tale.
Listen close, you might just find,
Whispers carried by the kind.

Tapestry of Tender Emotions

Threads of gold and silver spun,
Woven tales of hearts now run.
In each knot, a story glows,
In gentle hues, the passion flows.

Beautiful patterns intertwine,
Softly melding, yours and mine.
Every stitch a heartfelt sigh,
Shared in silence, you and I.

Moments captured, shadows cast,
Echoes of a love that lasts.
In this fabric, truths collide,
A tapestry where dreams reside.

Fingers trace the edges fine,
In this creation, love entwines.
Each emotion, layered deep,
A sacred bond we vow to keep.

A Hush Between Two Beating Hearts

In the quiet, whispers meet,
Two lives dancing, soft and sweet.
Silent vows in shadows lie,
With every breath, a gentle sigh.

Eyes that speak without a sound,
In this stillness, love is found.
Moments shared, a secret place,
Where time slows in our embrace.

Fingers brush—a fleeting touch,
In this hush, we feel so much.
Harmony in silence flows,
In this space, our heartbeat grows.

Two souls blend, a tender art,
Every pulse, a loyal part.
In the quiet, love imparts,
A hush sealing two beating hearts.

Lanterns of Inner Understanding

Glowing softly in the night,
Lanterns whisper, casting light.
Paths of wisdom softly gleam,
Guiding souls to shared esteem.

Light reveals the hidden truths,
In the stillness, seek the roots.
Every glow a story told,
Of warmth and courage, fierce and bold.

Together we illuminate,
Lessons learned, we celebrate.
Each flicker, an embrace divine,
In this glow, your hand in mine.

Lanterns dance on winds of change,
In understanding, we rearrange.
Holding close what lights our way,
In the dark, hope will not sway.

A Dance with Vulnerability

In shadows we often hide,
Yet strength lies deep inside.
With every step, we learn to trust,
In openness, we find the rust.

A gentle hand, a fragile heart,
In the dance, we play our part.
With each stumble, we break the chain,
A tapestry woven from joy and pain.

Together we face the darkest fears,
With laughter that washes away the tears.
In vulnerability, we find our grace,
Connected souls in this sacred space.

So let us twirl under the stars,
With our wounds, we'll wear our scars.
For in this dance, we come alive,
Embracing the truth that helps us thrive.

The Language of Warmth

Words can wrap like a soft embrace,
Creating a safe and gentle space.
In the silence, warmth can grow,
Binding hearts in the flow of glow.

A smile shared, a glance sincere,
In these moments, love draws near.
With laughter bubbling like a stream,
We weave together a tender dream.

Kindness spoken, softly expressed,
In every word, we are blessed.
Like sunlight breaking through the shade,
Our language of warmth will never fade.

So let us speak with hearts aligned,
In this symphony, we find.
A melody woven from love's decree,
In the language of warmth, we are free.

Reflections of a Kindred Soul

In the mirror, I see your gaze,
A connection that sets ablaze.
Like stars that twinkle in the night,
Two hearts dance in shared delight.

Through whispered secrets, we confide,
In our laughter, we take pride.
With every moment, memories bloom,
In the spaces where love finds room.

When shadows fall and doubt draws near,
Your voice a comfort, pure and clear.
A kindred spirit, hand in hand,
Together, we rise, together we stand.

In the tapestry of time and fate,
Our souls entwine, forever sate.
For in your eyes, I find my home,
In reflections shared, we are never alone.

Beneath the Surface of Silence

In quiet moments, whispers dwell,
A secret language we can tell.
Beneath the calm, a storm may brew,
Yet in the stillness, love shines through.

Eyes that speak without a sound,
In silence, our hearts are found.
With gentle breaths, we share our fears,
In this hush, the truth appears.

Every pause holds a tale untold,
In the warmth of silence, we are bold.
Embracing words left unexpressed,
In this sanctuary, we're truly blessed.

So let the silence wrap us tight,
In every shadow, there is light.
For beneath the surface, love will rise,
In the quiet, we find our ties.

Embracing the Spaces Between

In quiet moments where silence grows,
We find the whispers only truth knows.
Between the lines of what we say,
Love lingers softly, guiding the way.

The spaces cradle hopes and fears,
Embracing laughter, harboring tears.
Glimmers of light in overlooked seams,
Weaving connections, stitching our dreams.

Each breath a bridge, each sigh a song,
In the stillness, we know we belong.
Hands reach out, hearts beat in time,
In the gaps, we find our rhyme.

So let us cherish the pause between,
In the quiet corners, life's truly seen.
For in the void where we often drift,
Lies the essence of love, our greatest gift.

A Winter's Tale of Gentle Understanding

Snowflakes dance on a tranquil eve,
Each one unique, a gift to believe.
In the chill, we hug our coats tight,
Yet find warmth in the soft glow of light.

Footprints follow, stories in lace,
The world a canvas, a frozen embrace.
With every breath, clouds whisper low,
In winter's hush, we learn to grow.

Fires crackle, shadows waltz on the wall,
We gather closely, answering the call.
Stories shared in the flickering glow,
Hearts open wide as the cold winds blow.

In this tale where silence reigns,
We find understanding, release our chains.
Hand in hand, beneath the moon's grace,
Love blossoms gently, in winter's embrace.

Stitches in the Quilt of Warmth

Together we gather, threads intertwine,
Creating a tapestry, rich and divine.
With each small stitch, a memory sewn,
Crafting a quilt of love fully grown.

Faded patterns tell stories of old,
Whispers of laughter, warmth to behold.
In patches of color, life's moments align,
Embraced by the fabric, the heart knows its sign.

Through trials and tears, the quilt holds it tight,
A blanket of comfort, a beacon of light.
Stitches of kindness in every seam,
We wrap ourselves up in this shared dream.

And as seasons shift, our quilt will expand,
With new love and joy stitched by hand.
In this creation, we find our worth,
A testament of warmth, a map of our hearth.

The Light That Connects Us All

Beneath the vast and starry sky,
A spark ignites, a gentle sigh.
In every heart, a flicker remains,
The light of love through joys and pains.

Strangers meet with silent grace,
A shared glance in time and space.
Unseen threads pull us near,
In every smile, we feel no fear.

Radiant hope in worlds apart,
Each moment shared, a beating heart.
In the darkest hours, we find the call,
Together we shine, the light connects us all.

So let us nurture this flame we hold,
In unity's warmth, let stories unfold.
For in the shadows, bright glimmers show,
That we are one, in love's gentle glow.

Sails of Openness

With sails unfurled, we catch the breeze,
Embracing paths that twist and weave.
The horizon calls, our hearts align,
In every moment, freedom shines.

We journey forth, with trust our guide,
Through storms and calm, we stand side by side.
The world unfolds, vast and wide,
In openness, we take our stride.

Each whisper of wind inspires our fate,
An adventure shared, we celebrate.
With laughter bright, our spirits soar,
In the dance of life, we seek much more.

So hoist the sails, let courage lead,
With hearts aglow, sow love's bright seed.
Together we'll navigate the tide,
In the sails of openness, we abide.

The Radiance of Genuine Care

In gentle gestures, kindness ignites,
A soothing balm in restless nights.
With every word, a bridge we build,
The heart's warm glow, our spirits thrilled.

Through trials faced, we stand as one,
In shared laughter, life's battles won.
An honest glance, a tender touch,
In the radiance of care, we thrive so much.

Each moment cherished, a treasure found,
In compassion's light, our love is crowned.
A tapestry of souls entwined,
In genuine care, our hearts aligned.

Together we rise, through joy and strife,
Illuminated, this precious life.
In the warmth of love, our spirits share,
A luminous glow, the gift of care.

Mosaics of Shared Experience

In colors bright, our stories blend,
Each life's a piece that we commend.
With every tear, and every smile,
Mosaics form, our hearts compile.

Through laughter's echo and sorrow's space,
A tapestry we weave, embrace.
In every moment, together we stand,
Creating art, both bold and grand.

Each thread we share, rich and deep,
Keeps memories alive, our connections keep.
In moments captured, our truth is shown,
In shared experience, we are not alone.

So let us gather, let stories flow,
In vibrant shades, our spirits grow.
A masterpiece of life laid bare,
In the mosaics of time, we always care.

Wellspring of Insight

Deep within, a fountain flows,
Where wisdom dances, and knowing grows.
In silent whispers, the truth awaits,
A wellspring's gift, as the heart creates.

Through every question, we seek the light,
In shadows cast, we find our sight.
In moments still, when thoughts align,
Insight unfolds, so pure, so fine.

With open minds, we explore the maze,
Each lesson learned, a fire that blazes.
In the depths of silence, we find our way,
A journey of thoughts, come what may.

So drink from the well, let knowledge flow,
In the wellspring of insight, our spirits glow.
With every drop, we grow and learn,
In the heart of knowing, our souls turn.

Threads of Compassion Woven Deep

In the warmth of a gentle touch,
Hearts open wide, feeling so much.
A bridge built strong with love and care,
We find our strength when we share.

A whisper carried on the breeze,
Understanding flows with such ease.
We stitch our stories, hand in hand,
Creating bonds that truly stand.

Through trials faced, we gather near,
In silent strength, we conquer fear.
With every act of kindness shown,
We weave a fabric, warmly grown.

Together, we will rise and shine,
A tapestry of hearts aligned.
Threads of compassion woven deep,
In every promise that we keep.

Beneath the Surface of Still Waters

Calm reflects the heavens above,
Yet whispers hold the tales of love.
With every ripple, stories flow,
In silence, secrets softly glow.

Beneath the surface, thoughts collide,
Dreams and fears cannot abide.
Mysteries sleep in the depths below,
Yearning for a light to grow.

The moonlight dances on the lake,
Guiding the path that we will take.
With every breath, we dive in deep,
Finding treasures that we keep.

In stillness, we discover truth,
The echoes of our vibrant youth.
Beneath the surface, peace resides,
Embraced by waters that confide.

Colors of a Silent Journey

Each step we take in quiet grace,
A journey through the vastest space.
With every hue, we paint our way,
In colors bold, we find our play.

Shades of azure, warmth of gold,
Stories whispered, yet untold.
Around each corner, new sights gleam,
In silent steps, we chase a dream.

Through forests deep and mountains high,
Beneath the vast, unending sky.
Nature's palette brings us peace,
In every heartbeat, sweet release.

Together, we traverse this land,
With hearts entwined, and hands unplanned.
Colors of a silent journey weave,
The tapestry of all we believe.

Murmurs of an Intuitive Spirit

In shadows deep, we sense the call,
A whispering wind that stirs us all.
The world around us bursts with sound,
In quiet moments, truths are found.

Murmurs dance upon the night,
Guiding us to inner light.
With every heartbeat, spirits rise,
In gentle glances, wisdom lies.

Trust the feelings deep inside,
Let intuition be your guide.
In nature's rhythm, hear the song,
To the path of self, we belong.

Awake the senses, feel the flow,
As through life's journey, we all grow.
Murmurs of an intuitive spirit,
Lead us on, and we shall hear it.

The Language of Unconventional Bonds

In whispered dreams we find our way,
Through the colors of the night,
With laughter shared in secret codes,
We break the barrier of light.

A glance, a touch, a wordless cue,
In every silence, a story flows,
Together we dance 'neath the unseen,
In a realm only we can know.

The world may not understand our tune,
Yet in our hearts, it resonates,
The ties that bind are strong and true,
A tapestry that fate creates.

In every heartbeat, love's refrain,
Unconventional paths we tread,
Through twists and turns, we forge ahead,
In this language, we are wed.

When Silence Speaks Volumes

A quiet room, a softly sigh,
And yet, the tension fills the air,
In stillness dwells the loudest truth,
Words unspoken linger there.

The weight of silence, thick and warm,
Cocooned in thoughts, we sit confined,
In every pause, emotions bloom,
A hidden force that's intertwined.

A glance exchanged, the flicker's spark,
A knowing smile, it says it all,
In silent echoes, hearts connect,
In absence loud, we hear the call.

For in the hush, our souls take flight,
As whispers float on gentle streams,
In silence found, we feel the night,
And craft our world with woven dreams.

Conversations with the Unseen

Beneath the surface, things unfold,
In shadows where our secrets dwell,
We share our thoughts with ghosts of old,
In whispers, they weave their spell.

The air is thick with stories told,
From places where the heart once roamed,
In every pause, a truth unfolds,
In depths of silence, we feel home.

A nod to distant memories shared,
An echo of a fleeting glance,
In unseen realms, our souls are bared,
In vague reflections, we still dance.

With every breath, connections grow,
Invisible threads that bind our fates,
Through conversations soft, we sow,
The seeds of love that time creates.

A Mosaic of Emotion's Echo

Fragments of feelings, colors bright,
Stitch together in a vibrant view,
Each shard a story waiting to bloom,
In patterns only we construe.

A touch of joy, a shade of pain,
The palette shifts, it weaves and bends,
In every hue, a chapter reigns,
With echoes of what love intends.

We stand amidst this crafted art,
With every heartbeat, shapes arise,
In every tear a brand new start,
A canvas sketched by longing sighs.

A mosaic made of life's embrace,
Through chaos bright, and calm so deep,
In every piece, we find our place,
Where echoes of our emotions sleep.

Emotions Woven in Time

In the tapestry of days gone by,
Threads of joy and sorrow lie.
Moments linger, soft and sweet,
Graceful patterns, hearts repeat.

With each tick, memories entwine,
Whispers of laughter, hearts align.
Time, a seamstress, weaves it all,
Stitched together, we never fall.

Fleeting seconds, gentle breath,
Life's rich colors, braving death.
Each heartbeat a story told,
In shadows and light, love's pure gold.

Emotions dance, a timeless play,
Guiding us through night and day.
Woven tightly, never frayed,
In our hearts, each moment laid.

Tides of Unspoken Affection

Beneath the waves, feelings swell,
Words unspoken weave a spell.
Softly crashing, silent sighs,
In the depths, true love lies.

Moons pull at the heart's deep sea,
Rhythms set by you and me.
Gentle surf, a calming grace,
In every glance, a warm embrace.

The shore awaits, where we explore,
Secrets shared on the ocean floor.
Drifting dreams on salty air,
Faithful hearts beyond compare.

Waves may rise and fall away,
Yet our bond will always stay.
Tides of love, a quiet force,
Together we will find our course.

The Resonance of True Connection

A spark ignites in the still of night,
Two souls dancing, pure delight.
In silence shared, we find our spark,
Illuminating paths in the dark.

Gentle echoes, heartbeats align,
In this moment, your hand in mine.
Unseen threads bind us as one,
Together we shine, brighter than sun.

Through trials faced and storms we brave,
A bond so strong, it's love we crave.
Resonance flows in every breath,
In true connection, there is no death.

With every word, strong and clear,
A melody that only we hear.
The symphony of life plays on,
In unity, we are never gone.

Quiet Echoes of Unseen Fortitude

In shadows cast, the brave will stand,
Quiet strength, a steady hand.
Glimmers of hope in darkened days,
Unseen battles, love's warm gaze.

Through whispered doubts and silent fears,
The heart holds fast, it perseveres.
In stillness found, a fierce resolve,
In every tear, problems dissolve.

Roots take hold beneath the ground,
Fortitude where love is found.
In each struggle, we find our way,
Together stronger, come what may.

Echoes soft, but bold in heart,
From trials passed, we'll never part.
In the quiet, strength is born,
Like the dawn after the storm.

The Quiet Power of Connection

In silence shared, two souls align,
A subtle bond, an unseen vine.
With gentle whispers, hearts embrace,
In this stillness, we find our place.

Through laughter light, through tears we weave,
The threads of trust that never leave.
In every glance, in every sigh,
A tapestry that will not die.

We dance beneath the stars at night,
With words unspoken, yet so bright.
In simple moments, we are whole,
In quiet power, we find our role.

Whispers of the Empathetic Soul

In gentle tones, the heart replies,
With knowing glances, no need for lies.
A kindred spirit, a guiding light,
In every struggle, we share the fight.

With hands outstretched, we reach and mend,
In shared locations, we transcend.
Embracing stories, both dark and bright,
The whispers linger, deep and light.

A quiet comfort, a truth so real,
The empathy in every meal.
Together we rise, together we stand,
In whispered dreams, we understand.

Echoes of Forgotten Dreams

In shadowed corners, dreams once bright,
Echo softly in the night.
Whispers linger, tales untold,
A silent yearning, brave and bold.

They flutter like leaves in autumn's breeze,
Flickering flames that seek to please.
In memory's dance, we see the spark,
Lost adventures whisper in the dark.

The past holds secrets, sweet and dear,
A symphony we long to hear.
In every echo, hope remains,
The heartbeat of those lost refrains.

Reflections in a Gentle Stream

Beneath the surface, ripples flow,
A mirror image, calm and slow.
Each drop of water, a story shared,
In quiet moments, hearts prepared.

The sunbeams dance, a golden hue,
In tranquil depths, we find what's true.
A gentle current, soothing and warm,
In nature's arms, we feel no harm.

The world reflected, gently sways,
In this embrace, we lose our ways.
Time slows down, a sacred stream,
In every glance, a living dream.

Whispers of Understanding

In quiet moments, we connect,
Words unspoken, hearts reflect.
A glance, a touch, a shared sigh,
In the stillness, we can fly.

Through gentle nods and soft gazes,
We find truth in hidden phases.
Like leaves that dance on a breeze,
Our souls open, eager to please.

In the silence, we build bridges,
Over rivers, through life's ridges.
Emotions weave a tender thread,
In every word that remains unsaid.

Together we find our way,
In the whispers of each day.
An understanding deep and pure,
In this bond, we find our cure.

Echoes of Compassion

A warm embrace in the cold night,
A gentle voice to guide the light.
In struggles shared, a bond so tight,
Compassion glows, a beacon bright.

With hands outstretched, we heal the pain,
Through shared laughter, joy can reign.
In every tear, a chance to grow,
In every heart, compassion flows.

We walk together, side by side,
In life's storms, we shall abide.
For in our hearts, the echoes play,
Reminding us, we're not astray.

Through every trial, we are strong,
United in a heartfelt song.
With love and care, we forge ahead,
In echoes sweet, our spirits wed.

In the Depths of Feeling

In the depths where shadows roam,
Feelings stir, calling us home.
Each whisper of the heart does sing,
Of all the joys that silence brings.

Through tangled fears, we'll search for light,
Finding meaning in the night.
With every heartbeat, love will rise,
Creating paths to brighter skies.

In moments fleeting, truth unfolds,
Secrets shared, stories told.
The depth of feeling, like a well,
In every drop, our spirits swell.

Together we dive, unafraid,
In the depths where dreams are laid.
For in this place, we find our way,
In the echoes of what we say.

Threads of Empathy

In each encounter, threads entwine,
Through every story, hearts align.
A tapestry of shared emotions,
Woven deep with gentle notions.

With open hearts, we learn and grow,
In colors bright, our feelings flow.
Threads of empathy, finely spun,
Connect our spirits, two as one.

In listening ears, we find our place,
Within the warmth of soft embrace.
As lives unfold, we understand,
The gentle pull of a guiding hand.

Together we weave, a stronger fate,
In every moment, we create.
For in this dance, we find our voice,
In threads of empathy, we rejoice.

Bridges Built by Kindness

In quiet moments, hands outstretched,
We forge connections, none can fetch.
With words like lanterns, shining bright,
We build our bridges through the night.

A gentle smile, a listening ear,
Transforms the dark, brings warmth near.
Through acts of love, we pave the way,
Creating bonds that will not fray.

When storms arise and shadows loom,
Our kindness blooms, dispelling gloom.
Together strong, we stand aligned,
These bridges built, forever bind.

So let us gather, hand in hand,
In this great journey, together stand.
In kindness' name, we rise, we meet,
With open hearts, we feel complete.

Luminescence of the Unseen

Deep within still waters lie,
The secrets bright beneath the sky.
In whispered tales the stars confide,
A luminescence, deep inside.

Through shadows cast, we find our way,
The unseen glow, it holds sway.
With every step, we rise anew,
Enlightened paths await our view.

In dreams' embrace, we search for light,
A spark ignites the endless night.
Through veils of doubt, we strive to see,
The beauty in what's yet to be.

So let us chase the faintest gleam,
In every heartbeat, find the dream.
With courage bold, we venture forth,
To understand our hidden worth.

Chasing Shadows of Knowing

In twilight's glow, we seek the truth,
Through winding paths, we chase our youth.
With every step, the shadows dance,
Inviting whispers, a fleeting chance.

Unraveled threads, like stories shared,
In shadows lurk the dreams we dared.
As questions linger on our lips,
The world unfolds, as time slips.

With open minds, we question fate,
Unravel mysteries, contemplate.
In silent moments, wisdom calls,
We rise together, never fall.

So let us wander where light bends,
In shadows' play, we find our friends.
A quest for knowing, hand in hand,
Embracing life's grand, shifting sand.

Heartbeats in Harmony

When hearts align, a rhythm found,
In sync with life, a joyful sound.
Each pulse a note in life's grand song,
Together crafting where we belong.

Through laughter shared, through tears we shed,
A tapestry of moments spread.
In harmony, we rise and sway,
Transforming nights into bright days.

As whispers weave through gentle air,
Each heartbeat echoes, strong and rare.
In every breath, connection blooms,
Creating magic that brightly looms.

So let us dance to love's sweet beat,
Embrace the rhythm, feel the heat.
With hearts in tune, we'll find our place,
In life's grand symphony, we embrace.

A Canvas of Intertwined Lives

In the heart of the city, colors blend,
Threads of stories that twist and bend.
A tapestry woven by hands unknown,
Each stroke a whisper, a seed that's sown.

Laughter and tears in the fabric of time,
Moments captured in rhythm and rhyme.
Lives intersect where paths overlap,
A canvas of memories, a shared map.

Through struggles faced, victories sweet,
In the dance of existence, all souls meet.
Unknown artists paint with the hues of fate,
On this canvas, love resonates great.

With every encounter, a story unfurls,
Embrace the beauty of our diverse worlds.
In this grand gallery of life we live,
A canvas alive, continually gives.

The Light Within Shadows

In the quiet corners where whispers dwell,
Shadows stretch long, weaving their spell.
Yet in the dark, a flicker ignites,
The soft glow of hope that defies the nights.

Amidst the silence, a voice can be found,
Echoes of dreams that linger around.
Light dances lightly, casting its grace,
Illuminating truths we often misplace.

Through trials faced in the depths of despair,
A beacon of courage, too bright to bear.
In the depths of the darkness, find solace and strength,
For the light within shadows extends great lengths.

So let us embrace both light and the night,
In contrast of darkness, our spirits take flight.
Together we rise, through shadows we roam,
For in every shadow, there's a call to home.

Resonance of Silent Thought

In the stillness of mind, where echoes reside,
Whispers of wisdom in silence confide.
Thoughts dance like shadows, elusive and fleeting,
In the chamber of quiet, where heartbeats are beating.

In the labyrinth of silence, reflections unite,
A resonance built in the absence of light.
Moments of clarity shimmer and smile,
As we navigate through the depths and the while.

Thoughts intertwine like threads in a weave,
Crafting the fibers of all we believe.
In the echoes of stillness, our spirits ignite,
The power of silence, a guide in the night.

So cherish the quiet, the whispers within,
For in silent thought, our journeys begin.
In the depths of our minds, a world to explore,
The resonance of silence opens the door.

Pathways of Kindred Spirits

Through winding trails where the wildflowers grow,
Two hearts walk together, moving slow.
Each step a promise, in trust we tread,
Pathways of kindred spirits, gently led.

In laughter and solace, our stories unfold,
Sharing our secrets, treasures untold.
Footprints in the earth, a bond made of gold,
A connection so deep, like a tale retold.

Through the storms and the sun, we wander side by side,
In this journey of life, our souls collide.
With every shared heartbeat, we learn to believe,
In pathways together, the love we conceive.

So let us embrace this beautiful quest,
With kindred spirits, we are truly blessed.
Through all of existence, hand in hand we flow,
On pathways of love, forever we grow.

Beneath the Surface of Sincere Longing

In shadows deep, emotions lie,
Yearnings whisper, unseen sighs.
A heart that beats, a silent plea,
For love that craves to be set free.

Beneath the waves, hope gently swells,
A story told where silence dwells.
Every glance, a tender spark,
Igniting dreams within the dark.

Through layers thick, we reach for light,
Navigating through the night.
With every breath, the promise grows,
To find a path where truth still flows.

So linger here, where feelings bloom,
In the quiet, find our room.
Embrace the depth, the hidden grace,
In sincere longing, we find our place.

Colors of Compassionate Reflection

In hues of joy, the canvas glows,
Each brush a story, love bestows.
Gentle strokes of kindness shared,
A masterpiece of souls laid bare.

Within the palette, rich and wide,
Compassion blooms, and shadows hide.
Every shade, a tale unfolds,
In quiet moments, warmth it holds.

With every choice, a color flows,
Painting bonds that gently grows.
The spectrum bright, yet soft and kind,
In reflection, our hearts aligned.

So let us paint with tender grace,
In the gallery of love's embrace.
For in each stroke, a light can spark,
Creating beauty in the dark.

Heartbeats of Connection

Two hearts entwined, a rhythmic dance,
Each pulse a sweet, unspoken chance.
In every beat, a story's told,
In whispered secrets, love unfolds.

Across the space, the echoes ring,
A symphony that life may bring.
With every touch, a tether strong,
Belonging found where we belong.

In tender breaths, we share a tune,
A melody beneath the moon.
For in this journey, hand in hand,
Connected hearts will understand.

So let us cherish every sound,
In heartbeats soft, the love profound.
For in this rhythm, truth we'll find,
A bond unbroken, intertwined.

An Invitation to Deeper Understanding

Step closer now, let's share our view,
In honest words, find something true.
With open hearts, we can explore,
The depths of thoughts we've yet to store.

In every glance, an urge to see,
The layers masked within you and me.
An invitation to seek the core,
To understand, to learn, to soar.

With patience wrapped in quiet grace,
We'll navigate this sacred space.
Each question asked, a bridge extended,
In conversation, love defended.

So wander here, where minds can meet,
With kindness cast, each truth we greet.
For in understanding, we can find,
The beauty shared when hearts align.

Finding Sunlight in the Rain

Drips of silver fall down slow,
Each drop a whisper, soft and low.
Within the shadows, light will gleam,
Hope dances lightly, like a dream.

Puddles mirror clouds above,
Nature's heart beats strong with love.
Amidst the storm, a warmth we find,
A promise of peace, unconfined.

Colors bloom where sorrows fade,
In every tear, a truth is made.
The sun will rise behind the gray,
Guiding us towards a brighter day.

So let the rains fall, let them flow,
For in their wake, new joys will grow.
Embrace the dance, the wild refrain,
We'll find our sunlight in the rain.

The Bridge Between You and Me

In silence built, a bridge of dreams,
Where laughter weaves through quiet streams.
With every step, connection grows,
A tapestry of love that glows.

Our fingers stretch across the void,
In every glance, a world enjoyed.
Through whispered thoughts and tender sighs,
We cross the chasm, hearts arise.

Though distance breaks the visible line,
In spirit close, our souls entwine.
United we stand, side by side,
With trust that flows like a gentle tide.

So take my hand, we'll walk this path,
In every storm, it's love we'll clasp.
Forever strong, this bridge will be,
The bond that thrives — just you and me.

Fragments of Unshared Secrets

Hidden whispers lost in time,
In shadows cast, a fleeting rhyme.
Burdened hearts hold truths so deep,
In silence, promises we keep.

Cookies crumble, stories fade,
In the dark, our fears invade.
Yet lightly held, those secrets lie,
Like fragile wings on which they fly.

Each glance, a hint; each smile, a clue,
In crowded rooms, it's me and you.
Words unspoken, yet understood,
In hidden realms where souls once stood.

Let's gather shards and craft a tale,
We'll find the light that will prevail.
In fragments shared, our hearts will soar,
Transforming secrets into more.

Through the Veil of Feelings

Emotions swirl like autumn leaves,
Each color tells of what it weaves.
Behind the veil, we glimpse the wild,
Where pain and joy are reconciled.

Shadows dance in fading light,
With every breath, we touch the night.
In whispered thoughts, our truths collide,
Through veils of feelings, we confide.

The heart a compass, lost yet found,
In tangled woods, our souls are bound.
With every step, a new embrace,
Through the veil, we find our place.

So let us wander, hand in hand,
In this vast sea where feelings stand.
Together we'll traverse the dream,
Through veils of love that brightly beam.

www.ingramcontent.com/pod-product-compliance
Ingram Content Group UK Ltd.
Pitfield, Milton Keynes, MK11 3LW, UK
UKHW030846221224
452712UK00006B/486